in the bowl of my eye

POETRY

keith garebian

MAWEN𝒵I
HOUSE

We acknowledge the support of the Canada Council for the Arts for our publishing
program. We also acknowledge support from the Government of Ontario through
the Ontario Arts Council, and the support of the Government of Canada through
the Canada Book Fund.

Cover art by Keith Garebian
Cover design by Alexis Di Maria
Author photo credit: Elisabeth Feryn

Library and Archives Canada Cataloguing in Publication
Title: In the bowl of my eye : poetry / Keith Garebian.
Names: Garebian, Keith, author.
Identifiers: Canadiana (print) 20220195862 | Canadiana (ebook) 20220195889
| ISBN 9781774150696 (softcover) | ISBN 9781774150702 (EPUB) | ISBN
9781774150719 (PDF)
Classification: LCC PS8563.A645 I5 2022 | DDC C811/.6—dc23

Printed and bound in Canada by Coach House Printing

Mawenzi House Publishers Ltd.
39 Woburn Avenue (B)
Toronto, Ontario M5M 1K5
Canada
www.mawenzihouse.com

for Michael and Oliver

CONTENTS

In the Bowl of My Eye

Author's Note

In the Bowl of My Eye is a radical departure from my previous poetic themes and aesthetic practices. I was never much enamoured with what is commonly called "nature poetry," because too much of it has been a conventional romanticization or sentimentalization of nature and its manifold bounty. I am not easily enchanted by canopies of butterflies, fluorescent fronds, seas of grass. I have sought to refuse familiar tropes of nature poetry by refusing to sentimentalize neighbouring lake, park, and road, or by imitating Mary Oliver at her worst, as by walking fields with dog and notebook or by smelling flowers or wet woods at early hours. Maturity in age and experience have shaped me to be a little more like a meditative Wordsworth; in other words, "to look on nature, not as in the hour of thoughtless youth; but hearing oftentimes the still, sad music of humanity." Consequently, I have looked closely at suburban neighbours, young and old, healthy and decrepit, diverse, neurotic, virtuous, flawed, joyous, disillusioned. Real people from real life, often crystallized by gestures.

In this collection, I interrogate myself in my suburban Mississauga world, particularly in the summative final two poems. This book demonstrates how mortality weighs on my mind, for I know that life never escapes entropy, and that we cannot cancel or "unbecome" pain. Thorns and dark shadows remain, but we can still sing as naturally as blood coursing through our veins. I can truthfully and justifiably claim that because much of what I write arises from the depth of intimate experience, a reader reads *the work inside me*.

All truths wait in all things,
They neither hasten their own delivery nor resist it,
They do not need the obstetric forceps of the surgeon,
The insignificant is as big to me as any,
(What is less or more than a touch?)

—Walt Whitman, *"Song of Myself"*

Prologue

In Barcelona, fires in the streets,
the general trance is death-fear,
uproar the only music,
the only certainty.
Wind and moonlight
leak through holes
of a ruined house,
and it is impossible
to feel fully human.

In Hong Kong, mass protests
against repressive tactics.
Already hibiscus and bamboo
broken   unable to heal.
Tyranny, a wild vine
attempts to choke a people
used to colonial ghosts,
yet multitudes refuse to be mute.

In North America, caught
in mass hypnosis by a tweeting
orange-haired hysterical fraud,
there are many minutes of silence
for the death of democracy.

And I live in suburbia,
no paradise or Sahara.
Suburbia, I know too well
"the kitchen bulbs

which blister your dark,"[1]
the cabals of housewives
sniffing out gossip,
"the claustrophobia
of your back gardens varicose
with shrubs."[2]
Yet somewhere in this place
windows open to
a brush of leaves over a road,
glints of sun on moving cars,
picnic tables laid out in a park
for anecdotal conversation,
a lake which organizes itself
as assorted birds dip and float,
stones with natural texts,
and humans unwinding themselves
where I can record voices
from elsewhere, compose poems
which will not beg forgiveness
in an age of cacophony,
for my measured solitude
in a site worn by unmarked echoes.

---

1   "Ode to Suburbia" by Eavan Boland
2   "Ode to Suburbia" by Eavan Boland

Suburban Portraits

I am of old and young, of the foolish as much as the wise,
Regardless of others, ever regardful of others,
Maternal as well as paternal, a child as well as a man,
Stuff'd with the stuff that is coarse and stuff'd with the stuff
that is fine...

—Walt Whitman, *"Song of Myself"*

Monday Watcher

Chinese widow
by a window
overlooking park and lake,
rocking gently at
the Monday world outside.

Grime mounts on furniture,
maids are cleaning for other widows
but she sits, watches
while birds are hectic in their trees,
bread winners surge to work,

yellow school buses load kids
loud with gossip about their weekend.
The window doesn't matter in itself,
but it is her favourite,
always something to see.

Her three children in Hong Kong
summon her to return,
thinking she is much too lonely
in her widowhood.
She rocks in meditation:

what shall she say of today?
There is nothing sad here
by the lake.
What she sees best is close.
To return where they need her
is to lose herself,
vanish and begin again.

She does not miss the card games,
mah-jong, tea rituals,
yum cha, casinos.
She does not mind the cracked
bathtub, or peeling walls.

Those wounds are not hers.
Her heart strong, lips soundless,
she prays to moving clouds.

Suburban Purgatory

The out-of-work males come in two kinds:
the plump youth who carries a briefcase
headed for an office job he doesn't have;
the grizzled middle-age twins, weekly beer
in tow, who live with their widow mother
in a sleek penthouse facing the park,
thickly green, notorious.

Nature abounds
as do lubricious gays
cruising the bushes and earnest cops
out of uniform, intent on entrapment.
The gays tempt luck. Excitement
of public danger, fleeting pleasure.
Do the cops wish to be more desired?

In suburbia, this is scandal,
suburbia being ex-urban,
pedestrian, minds as finely clipped
as lawns luxuriating in weed-killer.
A symptom, a condition
embedded, like shopping malls
only a little less tedious
than a small-town tabloid.

Malls, arenas, beer stores,
veterans' lodge, inevitable
townhouse with numbered parking spots,
schools with a little learning, accidental value
interspersed with psychotic incidents,
mimetic gestures from disappointing lives
yearning to be managed digitally.

Surveillance

Summer. The road has potholes,
small graves, but the lake is not a risen killer.
A moving van arrives to load a family's furniture,
the sheer mass of belongings making me wonder
what a machine can suck out of crevices.
A courier on the surveillance video
scans the lobby directory. I try to guess
from the size of his packages
who gets what and why.

Then, what to have for lunch
as old Nerissa, Black widow on the 14th,
wends her patient way to No Frills.
In her solitary life,
she's a steadfast Christian, steeped
in prayerful optimism.

Dormant pots of artificial flowers on the 17th
can't tempt the birds, who like a real hanging
plant, its corded bowl useful for a nest.
The condo lawn neatly cropped. The little library
stuffed with paperback romances
on the ground floor hardly tried
by anyone who values literature.
An artificial fireplace opposite the elevators
exudes no heat, and the framed pictures
in dreary browns are bored with themselves:
scenes of darkest fall with bare black branches
are what no one wants to visit.

The Bench

A wooden bench, varnished,
in the front lobby. A bronze plate
reads: In loving memory of Frederick Ashby
(1913-2008) Irene Ashby (1915-2009).
Nothing more.
I remember him slumped over the steering wheel
of his small red car in the indoor garage.
Passenger-side door open as if
he had meant to step out.
He looked dead, but had merely fallen
asleep with exhaustion.
The car had a huge dent, front side.
When we had passed each other in the building,
he was already gravely stooped, as if bent
on touching the floor with his age.
Had a thin moustache, gone grey,
and smiled weakly.
A long-lived scrawny plant
drying out in its pot.

The condo posted a brief notice of his passing,
as if he had gone on a long journey somewhere remote.

I don't recall his widow.
Perhaps she was long invalided.
Chronic recluse. Or perhaps I missed her
as she waited, always waited for death,
postponing hers a year after his.

Their absent children donated the bench,

a place to pause and sit,
as outside, people rush over the small bridge
with the gurgling creek under.

Spinster Émigré

fruit torn swiftly from a limb
wind shaking dry bushes
rip in old fabric
distress siren
a mind tightening with each story she spins.
Life is erratic, she taken down by it.
Always looking back
at a door opening on more agitation.
The surging flood in her apartment, ornate with ormolu,
the gleaming white car she was tricked into buying,
the new refrigerator, overpriced,
instant calamity, dishonoured warranty.
Her complaints cause vertigo to her captive listeners,
surge like wild water impossible to tame.

Tranny

Heavy black truck
parked in the underground,
weekly haul of beer and wine,
muscular hands,
masculine face with deep blue eyes,
a smile to charm the dust off a rose.

His third wife is blind, pricking the floor
with a white cane,
fumbling for the mailbox key,
brailling the elevator buttons for the right floor.
Can't help turning a blind eye
to her spouse, of course,
who has retired from long-haul road trips,
his heart, two attacks later, no longer up to it.

Can she sense his mind on another gender
as they do it in the bedroom?
My prurience provoked by his appearance
at my door one evening
to help me lift out a stubborn window.
He was a vision in a long glimmering gown,
wig, drop-earrings, rouge, lipstick,
and low heels for comfort.
Expecting ardour, an invitation to foreplay,
he was met with silence,
wishing himself invisible,
his outré tranny display
drained like a leaking faucet,
drip dripping apology.

Evie

Her apartment adjoining mine
was always neat,
sign of an orderly life.
The old black cat seemed perfectly in place,
lapping milk quietly in a kitchen corner,
taking for granted the bowl of fruit
and silver toaster. It watched
her puff slowly on another cigarette,
coils of smoke keeping him from her lap.
No rush any weekday morning
even if her dry cough ruffled the air.

Sitting on her long balcony was too quiet,
lengthening the day before the noon mail
was collected, perused, sorted
into piles to be kept or discarded.

A glass of wine quickened her spirit
and tongue. No telling
what sensational news would slip out of her.
Television completed most of the day,
helped by the weekly *New Yorker* or daily *Star*.
She smoked while reading, through television time,
after meals. Nicotine her narcotic.

She sometimes misread things.
Cruising gays disappearing into bushes
of the neighbouring park aroused
her approval for their love of nature.

Nostalgia wreathed her at the best of times,
widow mind and heart forever wed

to a laminated spouse—
who had a secret fling in Europe on a business trip.
A sudden long-distance collect call
after they had curled into each other in bliss.
The mistress's breathy voice, anxious, uncertain,
Evie's storming against her spouse
put "Cancelled" to the affair.
Her iron will leashed him to her after,
his kisses for her alone.

His death did not mean he didn't exist anymore.
She raised a daily glass of wine to him,
held fast to her smokes,
did not seem to know
she was a thin wraith
the late night she appeared at my door,
agitation rippling quietly
as she asked if I had cigarettes to spare.

"No, sorry" was like a hand
withdrawing abruptly
from a friend's grasp
as the night thickened,
regret lumping in my throat.

Mumtaz

The living room your workplace
where you sewed by linty daylight,
repairing frayed jackets,
holes in pockets, drawing chalk marks,
cutting cloth, sticking pins,
perhaps wishing for the hearts
of Canadian voodoo dolls.
Hot nights, windows open,
air rich with the smell of curry
or stir-fried fish with herbs and garlic,
odours infiltrating seams
of clothes you mended
for clients from the condo.
Your head bowed by the Koran,
hoping what was to come
would be better than what
had gone before.
Your worn husband pacing back
and forth, clenching and unclenching
his fists.

The Old Lovers

Do they wonder about the length
of shadows, the gay pair,
time snowing their heads?
Do they still dream of youth
when sex, like light, was not in question?
The face of each in that green time
is lost in a pan of water, dissolved,
no matter how hard they look again.
They have learned the actions of life
are limited. Romance happened
in Sydney and Zagreb, birthplaces
of the old lovers. In Venice,
under and over bridges.
Paris, where they wrapped legs
around the Eiffel, devoured *crème
de marron* after duck confit.
Birdsongs were jewels.
Night was huge hunger for love.
They dreamed together after.

Came the middle of things,
when they argued about perspective,
exchanged grudging praise,
eyes wandering to other men,
other grades of quality.
They no longer hinged on each other.
Every July, Aleksander, the younger,
jetted to another in Rome,
bidding Alan "Ci vediamo dopo."

That "later" happened. Weight shifted,

sound of traffic grew tiresome,
cigarette breaks more frequent.
Aleks no longer frequented the park
across the road to sunbathe in the nude.
He took afternoon walks
when everything seemed to go silent.
Bewildered and tousled, Alan read
many meanings of "loss."
Spring was no longer what it used to be.
Each man learned to dream on his own,
tilting towards some place in darkness.

Habitat

Old mind-blasted Lear's
throne is a ramshackle Chevy,
relic of a better time. He
and his fool near a junk heap.
Poor Tom, naked, cold
in this landscape of refuse.
Sign of unaccommodated man,
doors and windows open,
yet going nowhere, except in their minds.

When I recall this stage production,
I think of some people I have met,
car-dwellers, their loneliness
paramour and doom.

The middle-aged Filipino,
cast out of marriage and home,
his battered suitcase in the back seat,
nights growing thick,
mind as brittle as his misery.

Or the gay Chinese couple
from Nova Scotia, one as bald
as Buddha, both muscled, huddled
in empty parking lots, inside their worn Toyota
in the thick of winter, perfect sign of banishment,
equal in their need for hearth and home
as the wind hurled across their car
more urgently than love.
Travellers with no fixed plans,
they worked as Imperial Buffet cooks,

rented smokers' rooms for a night or two
at Motel Six till their funds ran out.
Going nowhere, they learned habits
of displacement. Planning a future
was fishing in a dry gorge.
Yet they plotted out tomorrows
with the shared thought "Each day we are born,
each night we die again"—naked minds
designing forked reality.

Some Generations

Never the same happening.
Each recites its own story.

Ethiopian plump mother,
black apple face,
shrouded body in vermilion,
huge gold earrings, bracelet,
sandaled feet.
Four tall sons taking turns
in the gym. Her absent husband,
returns once a year,
never the same.
He hears wild desert winds, trees in tantrum,
hot rocks knocking inside his head
opposite the ultramarine lake.

The Chinese family of three.
Tall husband, blind in one eye,
his bird-thin wife with a superior mind,
lame in one foot, caused by birth,
not binding custom.
Their teenage son branching out
in two languages.

The Pakistani wife, with henna palms,
hostage to the Koran,
husband free of veils,
doomed by his birthplace.
He speaks an English some
refuse to understand.
"Why did I come here?"

Balsa-wood boat
on a rough ocean.

The lesbian Portuguese couple,
their middle-age love
a conspiracy against custom,
travel to many lands,
reaching out hands and words
like eager leaves reaching for sunlight.
They wander and wonder
among cathedrals, canals,
mercurial cities, dreaming
before they return with stories,
photos, new anxieties.

The older generations,
many tribes, many tongues
grooved like scars inside mouths.
no longer speaking only white.

The next generation a story
of a different happening.
Suburban young no longer rooted
in an impossible land.
Knowing tribalism is a hard ghetto,
they break free of boxes, bundles,
samovars and urns, rocking chairs
which travel only in the same place.

Wiry Vietnamese buskers,
two Sikhs on red bicycles,
Korean punks with tattoos.
Sri Lankan boys finger-pecking cellphones,
Jamaican youth loudly, proudly phallic.
All slough off family custom,

sabotage church, mosque, temple
at Starbucks or McDonalds,
sneer at words they don't experience,
know nothing of metaphors,
apocalyptic visions,
what to hope for
when asked of ethnic history.
"I will not become you!"
their gestures and feelings declare
to their elders.

Shopping malls, cinemas, and video games
their cocoons, they have short term memory,
brief attention spans, history limited
to a generation or two.
Their big arguments are about pleasure—
especially their vegetable love.

Their minds can't unfasten
from careless anchors, end their drift,
take root in something deeper than a whim
or selfish need—
the latest fashion, food, or fuck.

Suburban Mall

Some live a dull way of living very quickly and they are not then certain
that they are living a dull way of living.
Some are coming to know very well that they are living in a very dull
way of living. These go shopping.

—Gertrude Stein

Never close enough for some of the yellow homes
floating amid clipped green lawns
smooth as billiard tables,
the mall is an air-conditioned hive.
Busy shoppers come on wheels
as quick as winged gods,
equipped with magic plastic,
swift elixir of commodity.
Bodies gliding in silk or cotton,
legs strut on gleaming tile,
faces show a grid of whims,
excitement surging for special sales.
A calculated turning of the mind
to fulfill yearning at a price
that is not too much to pay.
Consumer love floats
across clean architecture.
They move, they compile:
new jewellery, leather, deodorant.
They stalk the aisles, bargain bins
where knots of pleasure grow.
Minds are tossing money. Best intentions
clamour in monologues with themselves.
What would Martha Stewart do?
Hesitation is mortal sin.
Bright lipstick eliminates

doubt, so does Chanel.
Bliss is everywhere,
swaggering to tomorrow
in fleece, gold and guiltless.

No Frills Coyote

Cruises the parking lot
at No Frills, stalking hidden,
shy, or frightened winter prey,
calculates strategy sneakily,
furry flanks smelling of wild,
dreaming blood-red meat.
Moves between parked cars,
mothers huddling kids who mistake
him for a lost pet dog.

Even men dodge his path,
hurrying away from omens.
Coldly trained trickster eyes
on Anishinaabe land. Lover,
glutton, demiurge, bringer of fire
and daylight which now streams pale.
Could have been early man, greedy
deceiver, concupiscent adulterer.
Would like to show us a special
trick of returning from the dead,
if we trust his passion which can rise
choir-high, half orgasmic,
full throated. A wooing you
must hasten to disinvite.

Getting Up

Morning drags itself out of sun reach
in freezing February when everything
seems reluctant to awake. The nested
birds, school kids, senior invalids
in the building on Lakeshore Road East.
As pink dawn runs to sullen grey
sky and clouds stumble, trucks grumble
and groan, heavy with freight, couriers
linger long on lobby buzzers, grateful
for short surcease on numbness.
The condo posts notices behind glass:
another water shutdown this week
to fix leaking pipes; warnings about
trash left in the underground parking;
more renovation on exterior brick façade.

At City Hall, a few miles up Burnhamthorpe,
the mayor and her councillors are voting
on another tax hike, as the price of gas
shoots up while the mercury keeps dropping.
Not much to look forward to. Spring is far
from sight. The only hope is an unexpected
heat wave: anything above zero.

Another elevator goes out of service,
but the old must keep patient going up
or down to garbage room, mail box,
or outdoors. The future tense for them
is probably short. Better to get up,
knowing they are on the edge of it.

Teen Suicide

Jimmy, 18, shy, smiling
stud, penis dangling,
designer gem under faded
jeans. Hooked on girls
he romanced, downing them,
drinking their praise
for his versatile tongue.
The girl he wanted most
shrugged him off, leaving
him empty, his runaway love.
Teen head buzzing, he left
a neighbour voice mail:
"Please call me soon."
His pleas a terrible shame.
In the bedroom echoing
quick strokes of young lust,
was rope strong enough
to crush his neck
like a strangled dream.

Soundscape

Heavy furniture scraping wooden floor,
thuds and screeches back and forth
above me. Spirit of work or restless anxiety,
perhaps some ghost intent on mischief.
Then thuds and sharp scrapings
of metal, machine heavy with labour.
It presses into metal angrily.
A hole or insignia. A button.
One does not matter. Another may.
Not I, not I, the impressed victim cries
in the stamp of time. The machine vents.
Not I, not I. The same retort. Repetition
matters in this world-jamming silence.
Mad stuff, the machine mouth part
of all the moving. My ears become eyes
fixed on the mystery forced into a cycle.

When the stamping stops, footfalls.
When the tread is light, a woman's.
A ferreting around, one step forward,
then back. Otherwise a silent she.
Then a pause. Perhaps she is waiting.
Staring into space, thinking, hanging
onto quiet air.

Some nights a bed rocks
as one body pushes into another.
The cries are from a mattress, bed
springs, the heavy frame. A repetition
once again, tempo changing. Perhaps
the bodies shift position.

With that the sounds, the speeds.
A crescendo...diminishing,
violent hushes...silence
absorbed into tone. Something
dried up. And they are startled
into the present.
No other way to understand it.
Just an end.

Old Lady in Rocking Chair

She knows the sun shines because it has to,
its light clawing at her eyes behind dark glasses,
her bony fingers gnarled with arthritis
scraping the window as a lonely wasp
buzzes its confusion. She farts, her frail body
agitating the air, she smiles, less wretched
than the insect. Her eyes search, famished
for grey squirrels sprinting up trees,
imperious geese stopping traffic in the park
as they waddle heavily across a path,
townhouses glowing in their windows,
a nearby clinic where appointments are kept or broken.
Her rocking is gentle, in tune with her body
going quiet slowly, thoughts mashed in her head.
She rocks to the sun, rocks to the time of day,
time of year, her heart nesting with birds on their branches.
Respite from indoor gloom, the pain in her legs
that had brought her to so many tottering stops.
She will rock the next day and the next,
day after day, all remaining life long,
dust in her carpets, small balls of fluff
under her bed, rise, swirl, and settle again.
Sometimes she rocks till the sun goes out,
dusk the usual intruder when murmurs
begin in her head again, she wondering
when it will end, this slow rocking, for real.

Lake/Road/Park

My voice goes after what my eyes cannot reach,
With the twirl of my tongue I encompass worlds
and volumes of worlds.

—Walt Whitman, *"Song of Myself"*

Prologue to a New World

Lakes and spruce, Douglas firs,
snow-capped Rockies, pre-Cambrian
rock, Laurentian Shield,
this land younger than the one
I was born to, tells the same truth:
land births us.

My birth land was oven-hot,
days an open-air sauna,
nights steamily oppressive,
even the sea boiled on days
when fish kept low, knowing
tough lessons of survival.
Savage with slums, sordid
with old disfigured whores,
beggars, shit, and pariah dogs,
teeming with many-tongued eccentrics,
it was exotic to those who preferred
the margins, who piled up silence
as criticism of a land where
exhaustion and emptiness twinned.

I knew proud old rock,
red as sin, the long Ganges
and its worshippers,
ankle-deep in ashes, waist-deep
in devotion, caves of erotica,
lust echoing lust, yonis
linked to lingams.
The country's mausoleums, museums,
dead history, vast, veined in marble.

The externals were easy to memorize,
yet I had scant knowledge of place,
the land's stories of possession/
dispossession, something learned
secondarily in books,
not empirically, metaphysically.
We were the land's before it was ours.

More than geography, I wanted intimacy
with words to record my city's
pathways, confusions and contusions,
myths which came from mouths
trained in temples, to teach me
to fear nothing but myself.

When I entered a foreign world
my family thought it wanted, I entered
(marginally) half-baked fantasies,
ambered in sentiment,
with a shallow heart, adolescent mind
harrowed by ghosts of desire.
It was a frigid land in the longest season,
snow and ice its irresistible emblems.
Out of my element, trapped
in an ice age, feeling as extreme
as the weather, my mind froze
out the landscape, words turned
to stumbling soliloquy after
the body shovelled Time's weight
in snowfall.

Now, in a new season, I want words
which will not lie abandoned
like a log-jam in a polluted river.

Suburbia lures my eyes to open wide
to the savage and the singular
as my mind shapes thoughts
sharp as pine needles, cool
as clear lake water.

Nature Poem

City life largely
estranged from flora
and fauna, no noble savage,
I didn't write nature poems,
longing for something other
than a world thick with bird song,
tree breath, lake sheen, and the usual
benevolence/maleficence:
muddy brown lands
putting out green shoots,
geraniums bursting into song,
cicadas crying in the heat,
howling wolves in snow,
bright chimes of metal. I preferred
flickers and shivers of human
life more than garden, topiary,
aviary.

I saw mimicry in nature,
small things imitating
larger selves unceasingly.
Nature's language different
from mine, I learned how poetry
of the garden "tends to be enigmatic,
letting images speak for themselves,"[3]
metaphor galore, even in what was red
in tooth and claw. This abundance
extravagant in poetry.
Too much whimsy,

---

3   Susan Glickman, "F# Major, (Firelight Spirea)"

exaltation, sublimity,
too much supplication.
I did not wish to waste myself
staring at the moon, leaves
of grass, barn swallows.
Where the raw, risible,
reprehensible human animal?
Nature didn't care. Why should I?

"Everything is a good idea at the time."[4]
Maturity sharpened my heart
with my eyes. Earth's motion
and stillness could stir dreams.
Nature was not just a subject,
but life itself—anomalous,
absurd, austere, ample.
A life in shapes
close to me, palpable,
each seen for what it is,
in its own skin.
No need to go long
distances. The best
locus the nearest to home.

---

4 Jim Harrison, "Returning to Earth"

Lake in the Beginning

Lake is astonishing water, not an idea
but difficult. Makes a mirage,
stroke in the eye, stretch of crystal
glitter, blue hope
spread to nothing. Currents
on the floor, not indicated by motion
do not show it plainer. Water greed
makes the bottom silent.

Not a single climate to circumscribe.
Burning summer, spring's pale
hesitancy, winter's dry ice burn.

Female space, womb
without labour. Suggestive space
wants to say what beyond.
In the beginning, chaos
before creation.
A stoned God to make
possible readings
imagination cannot regulate or hold.

This exterior is not a national interior,
shows choice, colour, cadence,
human relations migrant and settled,
domestic space.
Read the lake over and over,
argue against the park by it,
a tidy green but not delicate,
and the long road outside,

history extant, weighable,
reaching my curious eye.

Views From Lakeshore Road, Etobicoke

On the exact southern border of two suburbs divided by a
   creek.
Train tracks running downtown to a station of disunions.
Newly painted worn apartments looking from afar.
Low-income dwellings never seem bored or boring.
The sound of traffic overwhelms the creek.

The Public Works Department fouls up rush hour.
To view this from my 17th storey window from where
I can see the CN Tower, the city's proud phallus.
Cars drive by the trees, lawns, veterans' lodge,
paying scant attention to memorial wreaths and monuments.
Pigeons do their feeding by shadows of the fallen.

So much depends on the view from a condo.

Across the park is the long lake, opening the eye again and
   again.

A Little History

The lake's history is old, continuing.
I sift my life out
from shards and questions,
trying to remember the first tribes,
extinct in a blur.
Little more said of them,
      remembered of their faces,
      dug up of their lives,
shamans gone with ghosts and magic.

Memoir

Binocular men are peering into the lake.
No border there, only waver or shimmer
of liquid light. The fish are deeper, borderless.

Nor does the young Filipino family have a border.
Delicately joyous at their al fresco picnic,
the father on a smart phone in Tagalog,
mother tending to the sandwiches and drinks,
son and daughter happy at their shadows.

Harsh sounds come from dogs unleashed,
chasing squirrels or flapping ducks.
Stories of their lives,
would be memoir of an afternoon,
when pods are falling
into patterns on the pathway.

Rattray Marsh

Rattray Marsh in early spring before the buds break
and the wildfowl arrive, is a lovely place
where the imagination can recreate the past.
    —Alan Skeoch, *Mississauga Where the River Speaks*

spent coral sunk in once-tropical sea
great inland sea birthing more life than the land,
crinoids anchoring stalks, torpedoing nautiloids
whose synonyms tentacle at least eight names,
coiled ammonites, hinged bivalves, scavenging

trilobites, fossils petrified
within a prehistoric system
overdosed on natural defaults,
long ahead of native settlements
planting three sisters: corn, beans, pumpkins.

our woods: lush chlorophyll prosody
in a divisible world, deciduous sugar maple,
basswood, oak, shagbark hickory,
ash, black cherry, ironwood, blue beech,
sweet and sour as poems,

conifers of pine, hemlock, cedar,
balsam fir, spruce, tamarack mourning
lost needles in winter,
shrubs of witch hazel, bladdernut, burning bush,
a bible before belief

codified into bristling bias.
pink underbelly of granite
beneath shale and sandstone,
Mississauga's ancient handwriting

we are still learning to decipher

through their long silences,
sounds gone under water, into rock,
sand, like shipwrecks.
what was once soft become stone,
mineral cache, colouring diagrams

with large sounding legends
to record where the created
go, leaving traces of mortality,
shine, shape, and sounds
which never come back again,

precipitates in a measure
of fatal hazards, history
of stony space, creation
confronted by de-creation
as the moon waits idly

remembering the big bang
and a range of rumbles,
bursts of fire and flood.
If beginning was the word,
what do we now hear?

Some Trees

some lure hammocks
some whistle the wind
some teach birds freedom
some are open air décor
some deepen mulberry summer
some log cabins thickly
some lean heavily above cattle
some age like tortoises
some weep in willows
some seed waters
some are skinned by storm

some teach about roots
some store stories in their trunks
some recite intimacy to lovers
some keep us down to earth
some spread darkness over roofs
some sentry the night
some shoulder the moon
some churn the symbolic mind
some thicken the vocabulary of form
some tell us of what is gone
some have nothing to say

Creek

You don't need a cold heart
to follow the creek, spilling
over rocks, vision inter-
rupted by the small bridge
dividing two boroughs,
till sun catches water again,
twenty yards farther,
ripples glinting, ducks
finding noisy joy
in pewter shallows.
Small creatures live
for simple things,
enduring what is cold,
remembering what it is
to thrive again
in earliest spring
in a new world.

Poem in Late Spring

The heart lifts in solitude,
eyes look to the turbulence between
outer contagion and human consolation.
Three families of geese, five goslings each
(teenagers now in brown cotton), feed
quietly along the lake's banks, deepening
green, the parents keeping watchful guard
against curious pets and children, as
late spring's light spills warm yellow.
Leashed dogs lead their owners across
the old bridge connecting one borough
to another, ducks paddling in circles
on the glinting water, gulls noisily
marauding scattered litter.
Where have the rare swans gone, I wonder.
Their seasonal visitations later than expected.
Perhaps hoodwinked by delayed spring,
they have glided the wrong way.

The park has come to confused life
after half a year's fearful constraints.
Threadbare bushes in the natural reserve
are putting out new green, fallen
logs alive with lichen, slugs, and mosses.
The paved pathway, rough with cracks
and sudden ruts, winds a curved corridor
of light and shade. Bicyclists, joggers,
strollers, mainly unmasked, no longer
in terrified postures. Air swollen
with freshness.
Raw nature bids us follow its lead.

A species different from it, we cast
smaller shadows, prone to follow
worn trails than make new ones.
There's safety in the tried and known.
Progress is left to well-paid city-planners,
sign boards announcing remodelling
of the park, commerce to the fore
in any mission statement.
The new park to look like a Disney
playground. Nothing to recognize
the larger cosmos in which man
is but a speck.

My heart is elsewhere, my mind
remembering how the creek turned
blood-red a month ago from a factory
leak of dye. That was one way
to add terror to paranoia,
already thick in winter's
wreckage, viral contagion.
No rhapsodies yet, but my apartment
windows open wide to light rushing in,
grass come to life again, sky expanding
its blue washes, as June prepares
to bust out all over.

This world the only one we have
we need to know in shapes and scents,
the way predators know prey.
But who the predator, who the prey
when time's stacked against our knowing
in full, habits shrouding us from what
we need to know through open doors?

Sky and lake stare at us, entering

our dreams as much as stars.
They seem to know what they like
about life, secure in knowing they are linked
by strings going down to the center
of the world, while I try to be more alert
about knowing and living in nature's whole,
recent months making the now and here
momentous with unease, a matter
of life and death. Time ticks away
in terse wisdoms we struggle to fix
in mind and heart, while life is passing,
this poem on the threshold of my tongue.

Queen Anne's Lace

They know themselves,
      learned something I didn't.
How lace and poison play tricks
as light slants on them.
Umbrels come into focus,
butterfly food, and their elegant
nets for trapping prey.
I contemplate perspective,
as likely to contain
warnings, wildflower benefits.
Sap burns, blistering human touch,
yet the eye is drawn to what looks virginal.
Not the last time for love and poison
in the same encounter.

Plainspeaking

(in the manner of Anne Carson)

Facts are, faces are. To forget these
is to cast rocks down a dry ravine,
disrespect time. And place—
especially the blue lips of the lake
pressing on fish and boats,
the long black road which seems
to have no end in sight.
Each day these teach me
a local language to write
about shapes—
spinal cord of sun, throat of moon,
slant of hard rain, sleep of stone—
tunnelling into faces, hearts
to reach buried ore.

Turtle

The small turtle struggling
out of a furrow is not accident.
Its destiny, suffering and survival,
I pass by, almost hearing
it forgive my witness far
from its memory of water.

Sumach

Green gone, red
clusters dye
bushes, topography,
boldness beating
the doldrums.
No longer hide
in woods where
poison's in the family.
In the cusp of winter
my eyes are birds
darting from red to red,
almost burned by flame.

Body in Lake

A dead man's float
in the lake, September
sunlight bubbling around
his shape sodden like emphysema.
A new death an old death
awaiting revelations.
Kids watch from the sand
and shingle, parents striving
to shield them from the sudden.
Clusters of feet watching it
be dead, ambulance and police cars
flashing lights, sun piercing
the lake's skin, no wind
to find the curl in wave,
but the mood hovers in air.
Lake locks its arms
around him, holding longer
than he had known before.
The bobbing body balloon
maybe going to burst,
leaving a riddle, how he came
to a place where he has nothing
to gain. A police vessel scans
the lake, wanting to know
what the water will tell
in its long body, dead man
floating over the deep.

Shoreline, Winter

Lakeshore east of Dixie,
road licked by maiden snow.

Balconies burlap potted plants,
snow on the ledges.

Trees in the park are bone.

Rodents breathe in winter hush,
countless plots buried.

Bodies swell with fat,
longer sleep in darkness.

Under ice, the lake
groans with age.

Sound too small to haul itself
from under.

Winter's End

Still world. A single
bird calls to the unseen,
wanting to express sensation
of something new,
never imagining how
its own sound can become
part of you, echoing
a human cry,
call cinched to cry.

Lake/Road/Park

Lake

Its water remembers the first canoes,
teeming salmon so thick you could walk
the water on their backs, alders marking a trail
far from broad banks, softer leaves dusting
the sky, wild fowl crowding bushes,
pigeons darkening Mimico after a glut of acorns.
The early water was crystal blue.
True virgins survived diving into the deep.
Tribes gave thanks this water could not be held
the way a hand holds rifle, money, or bible.

It remembers slaughters—fish by mills and machines,
pigeons by a storm of sticks flung to bring them down
by white settlers who could not abide black,
wanted them salted for market.
Green or blue is what the water wanted, not black,
not black robes baptizing the water, turning it dark,
stopping its singing of ancient songs, hearts
of Anishinaabe/Mississaugas shedding skins.
Before the men with wide-brimmed hats
and smaller minds arrived, fearing the waters,
branches did not break by themselves,
summer sank easily into earth,
Anishinaabe figuring things out on their feet.
Unlike the invaders, with minefield minds,
they did not wish to be certain of the world,
prizing pleasures in discovery—
sudden bend in the creek with two channels,
before rushing to lake water.

Seasons and their distinguishing marks:
spring staggering out of winter's hold
in melts and trickles,
summer's sunlit dance on water,
fall's paint reflected in shallows near the banks,
winter's tight white hold on the land, the still water.

In millennium's churn, sky and water no longer poems,
lake stuffed with crushed cans, reckless bottles,
factory dyes, struggles wounded
from its dying bed, historied out.

Road

The first silent paths spoke early history,
rough trails through woods, thick bushland,
shoving past wild nature's rocks and ravines.
Eyes seeding the land, sprouting crops,
expanding habitat, soil a divine drug.[5]
The road came, lengthening its skin
and tentacles, shredding what it could not hold.

Evergreens, hardwood gave it a name:
Long Branch, for trunks rising out of the earth,
limbs reaching like fingers, sap rising through leaves
to bird-nest crotches. The land an ark, sodden
at times, soft, spongy, full of things underfoot,
not necessarily in pairs. Tightening roots
cracked stone, showing nature abhorred
straight lines. And so the road dragged
itself in curves, pioneer feet adapting
like roots, hands building log cabins, saw mill,

---

5   Phrase from Wendell Berry's "The Man Born to Farming"

school and yard. Birds, butterflies, and bees
showed life doesn't travel along a road,
but journeys the rounds of seasons.

What the road taught was a story
of webbed lives, kinship with the fields,
reaching through ages with the seed. [6]
The past remembering itself in the present
of subdivisions, cottages, wharves,
ferry services, stage coaches, suburbs.
Man-made, hungry for the world.

Park

Hard to say how many shades of green
or red describe the day. Like the lake
and creek, colour moves. Green passes
silently from tree to tree.
Leaves, grass, bushes
paint the park, brush strokes firm,
colours moving over our faces.
Light inside the wood has a luminosity
different from the outside.
The sky's variable shades on a scale
of 1 to 10. Shadows on the ground
have a different scale, in brown or grey.

Colour isn't the only spectacle.
Numbers and silences thicken the park.
We can't count all the butterflies,
pinch all the worms, catch every grasshopper
jumping in the grass, hear all the notes

---

6 Phrase from Wendell Berry's "Rising"

of bird song. Innumerable things to show
time connected to movement, notice
the meaning of change. The park fills
with signs it would be cruel to waste
in light that falls on everything.

In the Bowl of My Eye

Space and Time! now I see it is true, what I guessed at,
What I guess'd when I loaf'd on the grass,
What I guess'd while I lay alone in my bed,
And again as I walk'd the beach under the paling stars
of the morning.

—Walt Whitman, *"Song of Myself"*

Nocturnal

Small trees of loneliness
dark with gay men, subterfuge
of parched longing. The moon,
silver apple, drips juice.

Odour of dead animal rot,
tangle of tree limbs, camouflage
of bush. Fleeting recreation,
sudden nakedness, splendid loins
not for love but risky ardour
to allow finite dreaming.

Night promises immoderation
after the first spill of seed.
The words of sperm on grass
tell what is done with loneliness.

Leak

Something pushed by something else
as in a story.
Captive to rusty pipes,
water yearning for a resting place
to spawn more water like eggs,
mating with dirt behind flimsy walls.
Matter struggling out of form.
The middle-aged piano teacher,
single mother on the floor below
the tumid invader, surprised in bed
by red or brown hemorrhage.
She cries, sound gendered, lifts
her night clothes, fears she will die
under water, night wound, breaking open
its hidden world to be at liberty.
Discovering her sleeping form, it pours
into her lap, pressing intimacy
upon her. Lonely, too, it has found
a way to put off its own loneliness.
Her lap becomes a mouth, water's
mouth opening on her flesh.
Hysterica passio. Down
her climbing panic, imagining
deluge, questions pouring out of her
about some god having a fit
of overwhelming love.

Picnic Bee

Quiet rhododendron, green walls
of leaves, blazing light on a couple
in foreplay under a thick tree,
his fingers massaging her breasts and shoulders
from behind, legs entwined with hers.

Mid-afternoon picnic, cool white wine,
sandwiches, our lips nibbled by butterfly
kisses, hearts inscriptive, fingertips
softly stroking skin.
Nearby rivulet looks cool,
grass at the edge of it, asleep.

While our tongues duel silently,
a zealous bumblebee does a busy
zigzag dance, startling my knee,
pricking the bubble of our sinuous
silence.

You gather damp mud
by the water's edge for a poultice
to ease the sting with cool
comfort, suck out the bee's
poison. I joke about this new
connection: I am putty in your fluent hands.

We are closer now, your touch imperative,
arousing as it becalms.

You Who Knew the Name of Every Plant,

every flower, shade
of every colour, what nutrients
should be added to the soil,
correct amount and time of year
to spread the seeds,
arrange the rows,
make neat borders,
kill weeds, re-invent
the backyard with roses
of flawless peach,
clematis climbing in purple,

didn't remember
gardens are within us
in their endless variety,
mine with calla lilies,
yours with chrysanthemums,
blooming a deadly fragrance
in our veins.

We smell of mortality.

As If

as if the garden with your prolific hostas
where our love flourished was dug up,
as if I left on assignment and you saw what lay ahead,
as if anyone does with clear eyes, unsalted

by tears of recrimination, as if the bedroom sheets,
the stains of love could be laundered, erased,
you hiding your antique treasures, the rusted
milk can we bought in Stratford, so you could

remove its taints, apply two coats of primer
as if love itself could be primed chemically,
or the gleaming finish for your dried flowers
were *memento mori* of a small planet

we both cherished a brief while, as if
under the white heat of wounding words
you could melt away without consequence,
knowing that things broken from one scarred mouth

to another is a story decaying, rutted
like a road beyond repair, blasted
by an ecstasy transforming all into piteous
fragments of what we each vanquish in forgetting,

as if you had forgotten the picnic bee
which buzzed its venom into my passive knee,
or the cool mud poultice you used to comfort me,
as if our erotic walks were never taken

know there's only scorn of flesh,
smeared mirrors, locked valises

stashed in closet corners,
the oppressor's wrong, the pangs

of disprized love, the law's delay
as we trample the brilliance
of grass and flower, look only
to gloom and silent rooms,

as if we suddenly turned inhuman,
eyes crystal only for no more world,
as if we are nothing more together
than small strangers under black stars.

Clematis

I've watched them long enough
through your speaking
of preferences, details
of gardening, purple
climbers, softer light
than in my gaze.
Your busy hands
working out problems,
mentally composing geometry,
where to plant other images,
balance colours, masses,
your indisputable expertise.
This is where you inscribe
clarity on nature,
not on me, difficult,
standing in the lower plots.

What We Knew of Love

After three years what we knew of love
was not the staring at each other
with stars in our eyes under moondust
not even looking in the same direction.
We gazed across a distance
between what we were and what we loved—
parade of lovers, spectres of baffled
infatuations, drained illusions,
sweetness soured.
All that history, never guiltless,
dreaming of ideals,
awakening at last
to our own natures.
Having learned we survive
at the expense of each other.
No longer face to face
intimately, we show
each other the empathy
denied in marriage.

Meditation

Does my building memorize the land it stands on,
the lake bed its broad water?
This land says I am a creature
caught in the toils of its love.

My mind learns intimacy with forces
we often shrink from, awed by their power.
It seeks a common language
with consonants of air, water, ice, earth,
charged with raw sounds, poetry of the land's
raw skin, air's conversation with water,
ice melting in the fire of summer.

Nature never ceases to hear itself
even as I grow a silence to reflect
on cartographies of progress.
When we wish to return to simpler life,
live like trees, distant blue hills, waving grass,
we are sentimentalists
who varnish the world we have desecrated,
wondering if the story ends
by fire, water, or pure forgetfulness.

Poem of First Lines From James Schuyler

this morning view
there are leaves
the light lies layered in the leaves
a wonderful freshness, air
an irregular rattle (shutters) and
a chimney, breathing a little smoke
a commingling sky
a few days are all we have.
      So count them as they pass.
all things are real
watching you sleep
books litter the bed
clean used ones, of course
dirty socks in dirty sneakers
the shadow of a bird
in the garden, sun

let me tell you
I do not always understand what you say
lying on the bed in the afternoon
a nothing day full of
a violent hush: and sunbursts
on a day like this the rain comes
in the sky a gray thought
the wind rests its cheek upon the ground
      and feels the cool damp
slowly
standing and watching
the scars upon the day

the day is gray
let me tell you
I do not always understand what you say
a few days are all we have.
     So count them as they pass.

Study of Lake (1)

Stretch of blue mind
over history,
floating past different cities.
Nothing holds you.
Light on the opposite shore,
repetitive yachts, foaming wake
churning on to fat salmon
for the great hunt in July.
Gulls peck rubbish on the thin beach,
sailboarders flapping
high above the water line,
curious traffic in the park
where leaves, bruised by sunlight,
tell me what they are going through.

Lake, object of ardour
as lovers cling to each other,
floating
above their shadows,
always returning to you.
Ears filled with sound,
shells waiting to hear
blue or silver clarities,
veils of water opening like air.

Study of Lake (2)

The best way to see the lake
is being far enough from it
so as not to disturb it
by close-up eyes.
No corner in it for my heart.
No heart but its own.
A creature enclosed in itself,
defined by itself, without conditionals.

Diamonds of light within
its lustrous water.
Sun polished, newly washed.

A mirror for natural nakedness.
Voluptuous revelations.

Entire emptiness endless.
Or so it seems
to the naked eye.
Lake is somehow a void.
Yet altogether in place.

Study of Lake (3)

Mind wants to believe
only what it can prove.
The lake has nothing to prove.
It is not interested in true and false.
It leaves man the mendacious creature.
The one who insists on finding a shape
for water, always surprised his mind
is a sieve through which the drops fall.

Study of Lake (4)

Plain water is where nothing takes place.

The lake is cold on the surface, unexplained below.

Who knows what slow trance awaits.

Water gets the sunlight first.

Sunlight pearls above.

The water dries fastest by the edges.

Water is woman: changeable, unpredictable. Its pleasure is conditional.

A Buddhist bows to the water, kneels, the lake demanding this.

If man-made, there is less to discuss.

Winter ice glints razor silver.

We fill the shallows with stone. Water gets the better of stone.

Some days, the lake looks locked in slate gray, water still, portentous.

A feeling of something beneath struggling to break free and rush upward.

Water erupting onto land is not a case of love. It acts sluttish.

Useless rushing to it.

We take our hungers to the lake and empty them.

Some bleed their sorrow into the lake, but the red is only sun blaze.

When we feel lonely, sorrow fills the mouth like drowning.

Poem of Deliberate Contemplation

"I hope it does not tell us an obvious anecdote
for none is intended."[7]
Summer having deserted its smears, I wandered
in the park in thin shafts
of cool, some damp. Middle hours
of thought. Where to find edges
of the lake, the limits of trees,
"past and future circle"[8]
around me in patterns of shadow.

My contemplation speaks, tenderly.
What human figures will wish
to be remembered
"after passing away from this world
where [they] moved as a frailty."[9]

I take note with my eyes for metaphor
but mention this only to myself,
avoiding sharp stones underfoot obliquely.
When metaphor is elusive, I feel
empty, pulling it out of me like tufts
of cotton candy nothing.

Such absence does not seek my consent.
Keep a diary, at least a notebook
is sound advice to live a true life
while recordings misgivings, errors
in altered linguistics. Everywhere

---

7   Edward Hopper
8   Anne Carson
9   Anne Carson

is difference, "haunted by the Derridean trace."[10]

Is this bumping into the world, into
difference, pragmatic, something
which has been done before,
therefore, practical from practice?

At home, in my crowded apartment,
a litter of books everywhere. Another
bumping into worlds. Ocean Vuong,
Salman Rushdie, WS Merwin,
Auden, Annie Dillard, Billy-Ray
Belcourt, Paul Celan, Atwood.
Testaments of thoughts I have had
or not. Epiphanies in embryo,
at least zygotes of shared language.
And the ability to be refreshed
by anomalies or paradox.

My books mingle abstract
with particular, present with past.
Why do you hold on to all
of them? I am asked.

Writing leads to more writing,
many re-readings. As Nature
is also read afresh each season.
Only Nature has no error breath
on the back of its neck, as we do.
I like "unlikely places
of confrontation," Carson's
attraction. To speculate

---

10   Karen Solie

and play in a wide field.
My eyes to loot the world's
treasures, my ears
to "hear the singing
of the real world."[11]

11 Virginia Woolf

In the Bowl of My Eye

All the bushes hunch together, lean trees
relieve hunger through stacked sugar,
late fall's violence havocs birds' nests
to an overture of cold rain, squawking seagulls,
geese lifting and arrowing together.
The city draws its mind across a grid of streets,
alleys, condos, and houses, all striving for stature
from intersections, vanity of maps
growing thick and overlapping.

A different light playing over trees
in desperation or mutability.
The lake continues everywhere, sounding
its own bed which we don't hear, chill
in the glinting. Salmon unfasten themselves
far out, navigating to their spawning place,
meta of what is natural, depth of instinct,
love of home in lustrous waters.

The wind cuts through
racks of tree limbs, black stain of rocks,
moves on all sides, shaking and remaking
shapes we thought we knew things by.
Meanwhile in the crux of this season
turning shabby as it swallows
the fires of spring and summer,
nature's mouth shows fangs.

These turns of season
a new text waiting to be read.
They take their own time.

Sometimes the hush of light
an exhalation, an almost
sigh. My eye intrudes, I smell rot
settling in—dead weight of leaves,
fallen branches, dry carcasses
of rodents, birds, roadkill.
The road outside the park goes on,
indifferent to us, existing as if
that is all it needs to do,
our footfalls impermanent.

Surfaces can be plucked, manoeuvered,
erased, but nature's tempo resists
my probes. Balcony gardens
can be shifted, configured, leaves trimmed,
flowers culled—not the sky in its changing
pigments, the passing hawk with red wingtips.
Like ephemera, we need to alter, patch
and re-patch our lives on this land
we like to divide into tidy sections
so we won't feel stranded.
Here is my new desire my eyes neglected.
Raw material, street, park, lake, environs,
and people who leave traces. Wish the lake
were transparent, not a broad blur.
Wish the park were in layers I could love
specifically. Wish the road could be
a kaleidoscope of a century, shining
even in the dark. And my voice more
than a wandering of body.

Sometimes, words detain us, objects
betray. When we throw our arms
around their images, what do we hold?

A sad unfulfillment,
a secret love, a wound?

I dream unity
in what I know of textures,
weathers, structures
issuing from a matrix
of everyday life.
One season tied to another,
like words of a poem,
fold upon fold, fond
fonts of time and its shadows.

The lake alone, the park,
the road, interpretable
at the end, repeating the
whole picture, nothing
in straight lines or fixed colours
to enter the bloodstream.

In the bowl of my eye
in front of my wide window
in the mirror sky
in the lake distance
in the scattered lights
in shadows on the road
in the reduced park
everything speaks
a language joined to my words
in new places where the knots
are tied.

Acknowledgements

"The Bench" and "Poem of First Lines from James Schuyler" were published in *The Banister (Niagara Poetry Anthology Vol. 33)*. "Suburban Mall" won Honourable Mention in the Dr. William Henry Drummond Poetry Contest and was published in the 2019 contest anthology.

"The Old Lovers" was published in *Thirteen (New Collected Poems from LGBTQ Writers in Canada)*, ed. Ali Blythe. "Monday Watcher" was published in *Old Bones & Battered Bookends*, eds. Ian Cognito and Pat Smekal. "Lake" from the long poem "Lake/Park/Road" was awarded Honourable Mention by George Elliott Clarke who judged the Love Lies Bleeding Poetry Contest of The Ontario Poetry Society, and was published in its contest anthology. My thanks to the various contest judges and editors of the anthologies.

Allan Briesmaster, Dorothy Sjoholm, Bruce Hunter, David and Rose Scollard, and Kevin Irie read this manuscript in various versions and made very useful comments that helped me strengthen the manuscript, so I thank them for their generous time and friendship. I also acknowledge the Ontario Arts Council and Mawenzi House for a Recommender Grant that enabled me to complete this project. A special debt of gratitude to Mike Douglas, Executive Director of the Mississauga Arts Council, and MAC itself for a special Career Development Grant. And, finally, but not least, deep gratitude to Nurjehan Aziz, MG Vassanji, and Sabrina Pignataro at Mawenzi House.

KEITH GAREBIAN (Armenian father and Anglo-Indian mother) was born in Bombay, India, and immigrated to Canada in 1961. Following his PhD in Canadian and Commonwealth Literature from Queen's University, he began his freelance career as literary and theatre critic, producing over two dozen books, two chapbooks, and hundreds of articles, features, interviews, and reviews. A resident of Mississauga, he has won numerous nominations and awards, including the William Saroyan Medal (Armenia) and four Mississauga Arts Awards.